This Book Belongs to:

Sasha Chiriboya

How to Be Healthy

Good health is being the best you.

You can build good health.

Here are seven ways to build good health.

1 Learn Health Facts

2 Get What You Need for Good Health

3 Make Health Plans

4 Think About Why You Do What You Do

5 Share What You Think and Feel

6 Make Wise Decisions™

7 Help Others to Be Safe and Healthy

HEALTH STANDARD 1 **Learn Health Facts**

1. Study and learn health facts.

You need 11 hours of sleep each night.

2. Ask questions about health facts.

Why do I need 11 hours of sleep?

3. Answer questions about health facts.

Tell why you need 11 hours of sleep.

4. Use health facts to do life skills.

A **life skill** is a healthful action you do.

One life skill is: *I will get plenty of sleep and rest.*

Do you do this life skill?

HEALTH STANDARD 2 Get What You Need for Good Health

1. Tell what you need for good health.

2. Find what you need for good health.

Find health facts in books.

Get health products from your parents or guardian.

Ask health helpers for what you need.

3. Check out what you need for good health.

Which one is better for you?

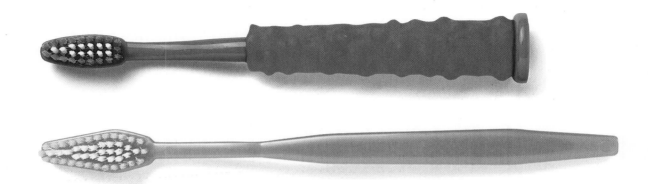

4. Take action when something is not right.

Tell your parents or guardian.

They can take it back.

Find Help if Someone is Hurt

1. Send a friend or yell for help.

2. Call 9-1-1 or 0 if you can not find a grownup.

3. Tell your name. Tell where you are.

4. Tell what happened.

5. Do what the person on the phone tells you to do.

HEALTH STANDARD 3 — Make Health Plans

A **health plan** is a plan to do a life skill.

Look at the health plan on the next page.

1. Tell the life skill you will do.

Life Skill — I will manage stress.

Name_____

Date_____

2. Give a plan for what you will do.

My Plan: I will do one of these things each day.

- Talk to a parent or guardian about stress.
- Get plenty of rest and sleep.
- Play with a pet.
- Get exercise.

3. Keep track of what you do.

What I Did:

Monday _I rode my bike._

Tuesday _I played with my cat._

My Health Plan

Stop Stress

Use the same life skill. Make your own Health Plan.

 **Life Skill** — I will manage stress.

Name_____

Date_____

My Plan: I will do one of these things each day.

- Talk to a parent or guardian about stress.
- Get plenty of rest and sleep.
- Play with a pet.
- Get exercise.

What I Did:

Monday	_I rode my bike._
Tuesday	_I played with my cat._
Wednesday	_____
Thursday	_____
Friday	_____

HEALTH STANDARD 4

Think About Why You Do What You Do

1. Name ways you learn about health.

2. Tell what things help health.

Tell what things harm health.

You see two ads on TV.

Which one is good for your health?

3. Choose what helps health.

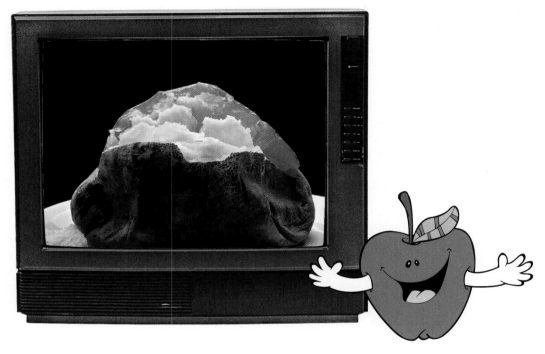

4. Do not choose what harms health.

HEALTH STANDARD 5
Share What You Think and Feel

Use Say NO Skills

Someone asks you to make a wrong decision.

Say NO.

Say NO skills are ways to say NO.

1. **Look at the person.**
2. **Say NO.**
3. **Tell the bad thing that can happen.**
4. **Say NO again if you need to.**
5. **Do not change your mind.**

Work Out Conflicts

A **conflict** is a disagreement.

You can work out conflict.

1. **Stay calm.**

2. **Listen to the other person.**

3. **Tell your side.**

4. **Think of ways to work things out.**

5. **Agree on a healthful and safe way.**

HEALTH STANDARD 6 | Make Wise Decisions™

A **wise decision** is the best choice.

This is how to make a wise decision.

1. Tell what the choices are.

Should you ride a bike without a helmet?

2. Ask questions before you choose.

"Yes" answers tell wise decisions.

- Is it healthful?
- Is it safe?
- Do I follow laws?
- Do I show respect for others?
- Do I follow family rules?
- Do I show good character?

Respect is thinking highly of someone.

Good character is having right actions.

3. Tell what the wise decision is.

4. Tell why.

I wear a helmet to keep my head safe.

HEALTH STANDARD 7 · Help Others to Be Safe and Healthy

1. Choose a safe, healthful action.

You play soccer.

You need some things to keep you safe when you play.

2. Tell others about it.

3. Do the safe, healthful action.

4. Help others do the safe, healthful action.

Say YES to Good Health!

Good health is being the best you.

Good health helps you do well in school.

Doing well in school means doing the very best *you* can do in school.

Macmillan/McGraw-Hill

Totally Awesome® Health

Linda Meeks
The Ohio State University

Philip Heit
The Ohio State University

Macmillan/McGraw-Hill

New York   Farmington

Credits
Cover Design and Illustration: Devost Design

Cover Photo: PhotoDisc

Photos: *All photographs are by Macmillan/McGraw-Hill (MMH); Roman Sapecki; Lew Lause; Ken Karp for MMH; and Lawrence Migdale for MMH, except as noted below.*
Front Matter: S1: b. Ken Cavanagh/Photo Researchers; S4: ml. Carolyn A. McKeone/Photo Researchers; S8: tc. PhotoDisc; tr. Peter Steiner/The Stock Market; bli. Michael Newman/Photo Edit; bri. Gerald Zanetti/The Stock Market; bl. PhotoDisc; br. PhotoDisc; S9: t. PhotoDisc; b. PhotoDisc; ti. Michael Newman/Photo Edit; bi. Gerald Zanetti/The Stock Market; S11: Tony Freeman/Photo Edit; S13: Bob Daemmrich/Stock Boston; S16: Richard Hutchings/Photo Researchers.

Illustrations: Jennifer King, Dave Odell, S.I. International Studio, Hideko Takahashi

Unit 10 outlines emergency care procedures that reflect the standard of knowledge and accepted practices in the United States at the time this book was published. It is the teacher's responsibility to stay informed of changes in emergency care procedures in order to teach current accepted practices. The teacher also can recommend that students gain complete, comprehensive training from courses offered by the American Red Cross.

learning through listening

Students with print disabilities may be eligible to obtain an accessible, audio version of the pupil edition of this textbook. Please call Recording for the Blind & Dyslexic at 1-800-221-4792 for complete information.

Macmillan/McGraw-Hill

*A Division of The **McGraw·Hill** Companies*

Published by Macmillan/McGraw-Hill, of McGraw-Hill Education, a division of The McGraw-Hill Companies, Inc., Two Penn Plaza, New York, New York 10121.

Printed in the United States of America

ISBN 0-02-280432-3 / 1

2 3 4 5 6 7 8 9 055/110 07 06 05 04 03

About the Authors

Professor Linda Meeks   **Dr. Philip Heit**

Linda Meeks and Philip Heit are emeritus professors of Health Education in the College of Education at The Ohio State University. Linda and Philip are America's most widely published health education co-authors. They have collaborated for more than 20 years, co-authoring more than 200 health books that are used by millions of students preschool through college. Together, they have helped state departments of education as well as thousands of school districts develop comprehensive school health education curricula. Their books and curricula are used throughout the United States as well as in Canada, Japan, Mexico, England, Puerto Rico, Spain, Egypt, Jordan, Saudi Arabia, Bermuda, and the Virgin Islands. Linda and Philip train professors as well as educators in state departments of education and school districts. Their book, *Comprehensive School Health Education: Totally Awesome® Strategies for Teaching Health,* is the most widely used book for teacher training in colleges, universities, and school districts. Thousands of teachers throughout the world have participated in their Totally Awesome® Teacher Training Workshops. Linda and Philip have been the keynote speakers for many teacher institutes and wellness conferences. They are personally and professionally committed to the health and well-being of youth.

Contributing Consultant

Susan Wooley, Ph.D., CHES
Executive Director
American School Health Association
Kent, Ohio

Advisory Board

Catherine M. Balsley, Ed.D., CHES
Director of Curriculum Support
School District of Philadelphia
Philadelphia, Pennsylvania

Gary English, Ph.D., CHES
Associate Professor of Health Education
Department of Health Promotion and
  Human Movement
Ithaca College
Ithaca, New York

Deborah Fortune, Ph.D., CHES
Director of HIV/AIDS Project
Association for the Advancement of Health
  Education
Reston, Virginia

Sheryl Gotts, M.S.
Curriculum Specialist
Office of Health and Physical Education
Milwaukee Public Schools
Milwaukee, Wisconsin

David Lohrman, Ph.D., CHES
Project Director
The Evaluation Consultation Center
Academy for Educational Development
Washington, D.C.

Deborah Miller, Ph.D., CHES
Professor and Health Coordinator
College/University of Charleston
Charleston, South Carolina

Joanne Owens-Nauslar, Ed.D.
President of AAHPERD
Director of Professional Development
American School Health Association
Kent, Ohio

Linda Peveler, M.S.
Health Teacher
Columbiana Middle School
Shelby County Public Schools
Birmingham, Alabama

LaNaya Ritson, M.S., CHES
Instructor, Department of Health Education
Western Oregon University
Monmouth, Oregon

John Rohwer, Ed.D.
Professor, Department of Health Education
Bethel College
St. Paul, Minnesota

Michael Schaffer, M.A.
Supervisor of Health Education K-12
Prince George's County Public Schools
Upper Marlboro, Maryland

Sherman Sowby, Ph.D., CHES
Professor, Health Science
California State University at Fresno
Fresno, California

Mae Waters, Ph.D., CHES
Executive Director Comprehensive School
  Health Programs Training Center
Florida State University
Tallahassee, Florida

Dee Wengert, Ph.D., CHES
Professor, Department of Health Science
Towson State University
Towson, Maryland

Medical Reviewers

Donna Bacchi, M.D., M.P.H.
Director, Division of
  Community Pediatrics
Texas Tech University
  Health Sciences Center
Lubbock, Texas

Albert J. Hart, Jr., M.D.
Mid-Ohio OB-GYN, Inc.
Westerville, Ohio

Reviewers

Kymm Ballard, M.A.
Physical Education, Athletics,
  and Sports Medicine
  Consultant
North Carolina Department
  of Public Instruction
Raleigh, North Carolina

Kay Bridges
Health Educator
Gaston County Public
  Schools
Gastonia, North Carolina

Lillie Burns
HIV/AIDS Prevention
  Education
Education Program
  Coordinator
Louisiana Department of
  Education
Baton Rouge, Louisiana

Deborah Carter-Hinton
Physical Education Health
  Resource Specialist
Joliet Public Schools
Joliet, Illinois

Anthony S. Catalano, Ph.D.
K-12 Health Coordinator
Melrose Public Schools
Melrose, Massachusetts

Galen Cole, M.P.H., Ph.D.
Division of Health
  Communication
Office of the Director
Centers for Disease Control
  and Prevention
Atlanta, Georgia

Brian Colwell, Ph.D.
Professor
Department of HLKN
Texas A&M University
College Station, Texas

Tommy Fleming, Ph.D.
Director of Health and
  Physical Education
Texas Education Agency
Austin, Texas

Elizabeth Gallun, M.A.
Specialist, Health and
  Physical Education
Office of Instructional
  Development
Maryland Department of
  Education
Baltimore, Maryland

Mary Gooding
Health Instructor
Tom Joy Elementary School
Nashville, Tennessee

Linda Harrill-Rudisill, M.A.
Chairperson of Health
  Education
Southwest Middle Schools
Gastonia, North Carolina

Janet Henke
Middle School Team Leader
Baltimore County Public
  Schools
Baltimore, Maryland

Russell Henke
Coordinator of Health
Montgomery County Public
  Schools
Rockville, Maryland

Robin Kimball
Belle Isle Enterprise Middle
  School
Oklahoma City, Oklahoma

Joe Leake, CHES
Curriculum Specialist
Baltimore City Public
  Schools
Baltimore, Maryland

Mary Marks, Ph.D.
Coordinator, Health and
  Physical Education
Fairfax County Public
  Schools
Falls Church, Virginia

Darlene Y. Nall
Health and Physical
  Education Instructor
Metro Nashville/Davidson
  County Public Schools
Nashville, Tennessee

Debra Ogden, M.A.
Coordinator of Health,
  Physical Education, Driver
  Education, and Safe and
  Drug-Free Programs
Collier County Public
  Schools
Naples, Florida

Merita Thompson, Ed.D.
Professor of Health
  Education
Eastern Kentucky University
Richmond, Kentucky

Linda Wright, M.A.
Project Director
HIV/AIDS Education
  Program
District of Columbia
  Public Schools
Washington, D.C.

Unit 1

Mental and Emotional Health

Unit 2

Family and Social Health

Unit 3

Growth and Development

x

Lesson 8 I Love My Body Book (continued)

Unit 4

Nutrition

xii

Unit
5

Personal Health and Physical Activity

Unit 6

Say NO!

Alcohol, Tobacco, and Other Drugs

Say NO!

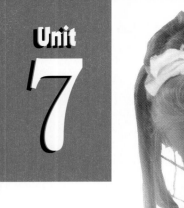

Communicable and Chronic Diseases

Unit 8

Consumer and Community Health

Unit 9

Environmental Health

Injury Prevention and Safety

Unit 1

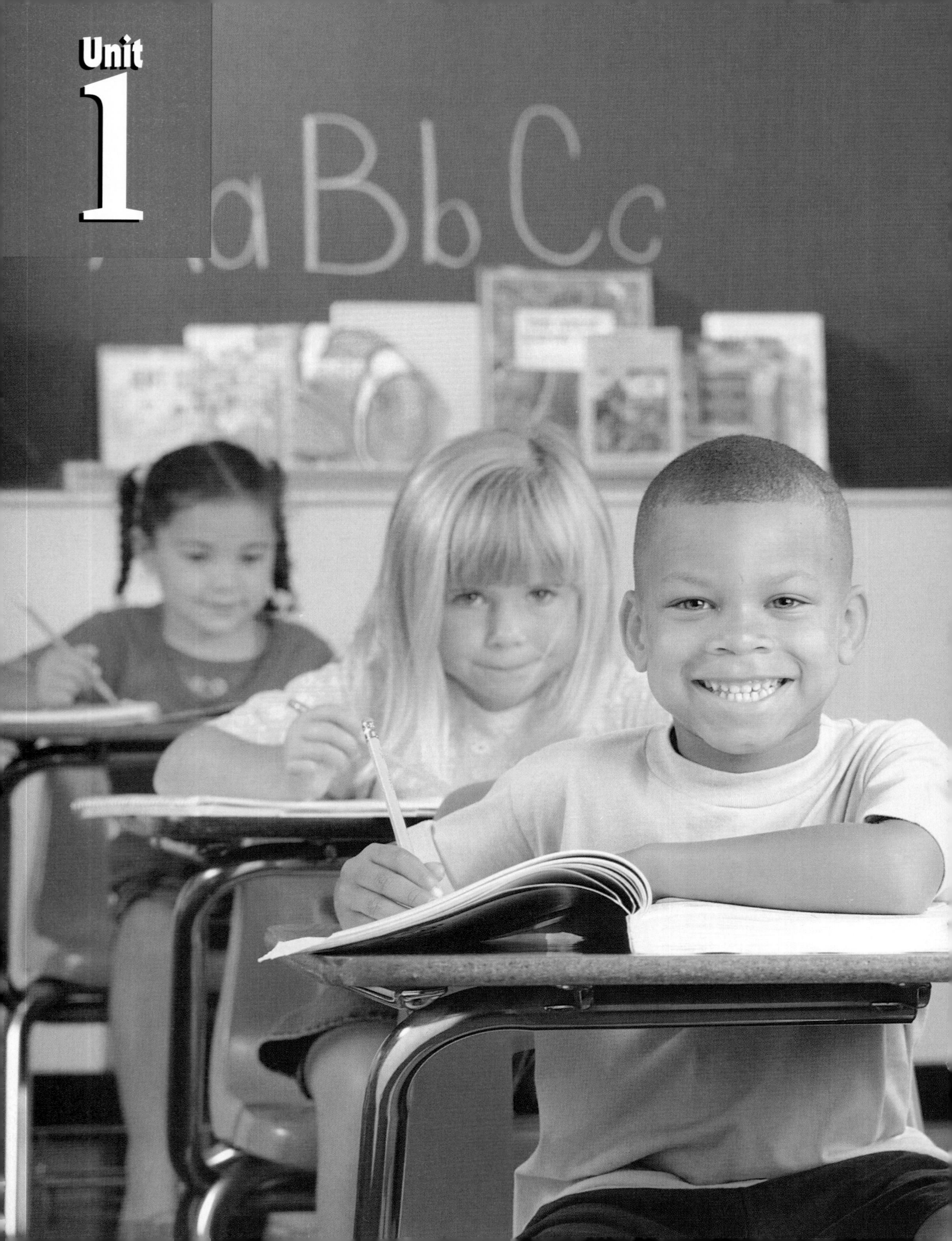

Mental and Emotional Health

Lesson 1
Health Puzzle

Lesson 2
Steps to Good Character

Lesson 3
Say NO and Mean It

Lesson 4
How You Show Feelings

PRACTICE

HEALTH STANDARD 1 ## Learn Health Facts

Practice this standard at the end of this unit.

1. **Study and learn health facts.** What does stress do to your heart?

2. **Ask questions about health facts.** Ask your teacher a question about stress.

3. **Answer questions about health facts.** Answer this: What can you do about stress?

4. **Use health facts to do life skills.** Tell how you will practice the life skill: *I will manage stress.*

Lesson

1 Health Puzzle

Life Skills

I will take care of my health.

I will practice life skills for health.

I will choose actions for a healthy mind.

What You Will Be Able to Do

Tell what good health is.

Tell when you should do life skills.

Tell how to make a health plan.

Words You Will Learn

Good health is being the best you.

Life skills are healthful actions you do.

A **health plan** is a plan to do a life skill.

What Is Health?

Good health is being the best you.

It is taking care of your body.

It is taking care of your mind.

It is getting along with others.

It is showing feelings.

What Are Life Skills?

Life skills are healthful actions you do.

You should do life skills your whole life.

One life skill is *I will get plenty of exercise.*

You need plenty of exercise right now.

You need plenty of exercise your whole life.

This book has 34 lessons in it.

There is one or more life skills for a lesson.

Do these life skills to be healthy.

I will get plenty of exercise.

What Is a Health Plan?

Look at the health plan on page 8.

A **health plan** is a plan to do a life skill.

You write out a health plan.

You put your name and date on it.

You tell which life skill you will do.

You make a plan to do it.

You keep track of what you did.

I will make a health plan to do a life skill.

My Health Plan

Use the same life skill. Make your own Health Plan.

Get Plenty of Exercise

 **Life Skill**

I will get plenty of exercise.

Name_____

Date_____

My Plan: I will exercise five days a week. I will choose exercises I enjoy.

- running
- swimming
- biking
- skating
- dancing
- playing baseball

What I Did:

Exercise I Did

Sunday _Dancing_____

Monday_____

Tuesday_____

Wednesday_____

Thursday_____

Friday_____

Saturday_____

Activity
Catch Good Health

1. Look in this book to find life skills.

2. Form a circle with your classmates.

3. Say a life skill you will do.

4. Throw a ball to a classmate.
   Your classmate will say a life skill.

5. Give all of your classmates a turn.

CATCH!

Lesson 1 Review

Health Questions

1. What is health? **page 5**

2. When should you do life skills? **page 6**

3. How do you make a health plan? **page 9**

Lesson 2
Steps to Good Character

Life Skills

I will show good character.
I will make wise decisions.

What You Will Be Able to Do

Tell ways to show good character.

Tell how to make wise decisions.

Words You Will Learn

Good character is having right actions.

A **wise decision** is the best choice.

What Is Good Character?

Good character is having right actions.

You can have good character.

There are three things you must do.

1. Tell the truth.

2. Show you care about others.

3. Be fair when you make choices.

What Is a Wise Decision?

A **wise decision** is the best choice.

A wise decision is healthful.

A wise decision is safe.

A wise decision follows laws.

A wise decision shows respect for others.

A wise decision follows family rules.

A wise decision shows good character.

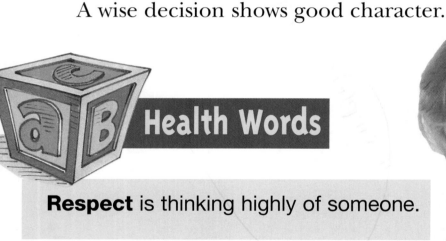

Health Words

Respect is thinking highly of someone.

Make Wise Decisions™

Ask questions before you choose.

"Yes" answers tell wise decisions.

1. Is it healthful?
2. Is it safe?
3. Do I follow laws?
4. Do I show respect for others?
5. Do I follow family rules?
6. Do I show good character?

Lesson 2 Review

Health Questions

1. What actions show good character? **page 11**
2. How can you make wise decisions? **page 12**

Lesson

3 Say NO and Mean It

Life Skill

I will say NO to wrong decisions.

What You Will Be Able to Do

Tell what a wrong decision is.

Tell how to use say NO skills.

Words You Will Learn

A **wrong decision** is a choice with bad results.

Say NO skills are ways to say NO.

What Is a Wrong Decision?

A **wrong decision** is a choice with bad results.

What if a friend tells you to cheat?

Bad results can happen if you cheat.

Cheating does not show good character.

Cheating is a wrong decision.

What if a friend asks you to smoke?

Bad results can happen if you smoke.

Smoking harms the heart and lungs.

Smoking is a wrong decision.

What Are Say NO Skills?

Say NO if asked to make a wrong decision.

Say NO skills are ways to say NO.

1. Look at the person.

2. Say NO.

3. Tell the bad result that can happen.

4. Say NO again if you need to.

5. Do not change your mind.

Say NO!

Activity

Say NO and Mean It

1. Take turns with a partner.
2. One partner will say a wrong decision.
3. The other partner will use say NO skills.

Wrong Decisions

1. Let's swim without an adult close by.
2. Let's skate without knee pads.
3. Let's hitchhike.
4. Let's ride double on our bikes.

Lesson 3 Review

Health Questions

1. What is a wrong decision? **page 15**
2. What are five say NO skills? **page 16**

Lesson 4

How You Show Feelings

Life Skills

I will share feelings.

I will manage stress.

I will bounce back from hard times.

What You Will Be Able to Do

Tell different feelings you have.

Tell healthful ways to share feelings.

Tell what to do when you feel stress.

Words You Will Learn

Feelings are the ways you feel inside.

Angry is feeling very mad.

Stress is body changes from strong feelings.

What Are Feelings?

Feelings are the ways you feel inside.

You have many different feelings.

You might feel happy or sad.

You can show your feelings.

Your face can show your feelings.

Your body can show your feelings.

How do you show your feelings?

One good way is to talk about them.

What Are Angry Feelings?

Angry is feeling very mad.

Do not do anything wrong if you are angry.

Do not start a fight.

Do not say bad words.

Do not break anything.

Keep your cool.

Talk things out.

My Health Plan

Use the same life skill. Make your own Health Plan.

Share My Feelings

 **Life Skill**

I will share feelings.

Name _____

Date _____

My Plan: These are healthful ways to share feelings.

- **I can draw a picture to show how I feel.**
- **I can write about how I feel.**
- **I can say how I feel.**

What I Did:

Sunday _I talked to a friend._

Monday _____

Tuesday _____

Wednesday _____

Thursday _____

Friday _____

Saturday _____

What Is Stress?

Stress is body changes from strong feelings.

Suppose you are angry or scared.

Your heart beats faster.

You breathe more often.

Your muscles get tight.

Your hands are sweaty.

Too much stress can make you tired.

You can get sick or have an accident.

I will manage stress.

What to Do About Stress

Talk to your parents or guardians.

Get plenty of rest and sleep.

Spend time with a friend.

Play with a pet.

Get exercise.

Lesson 4 Review

Health Questions

1. What are feelings? **page 19**

2. What are three healthful ways to share feelings?
   page 21

3. What are five things to do about stress?
   page 23

Unit 1 Review

Health Questions

1. When should you do life skills?
   Lesson 1 page 6

2. How can you make wise decisions?
   Lesson 2 page 12

3. What are five say NO skills?
   Lesson 3 page 16

4. What are five things to do about stress?
   Lesson 4 page 23

Health Words

Write the answers on your paper.

health plan
wise decision
wrong decision
stress

1. _____ is body changes from strong feelings.
   Lesson 4

2. A _____ _____ is the best choice.
   Lesson 2

3. A _____ _____ is a plan to do a life skill.
   Lesson 1

4. A _____ _____ is a choice with bad results.
   Lesson 3

Make Wise Decisions™

Your friend tells you to lie to your teacher.

Suppose you lie.

- Do you show respect for others?
- Do you follow family rules?
- Do you show good character?

What should you do?

Health Skills

Express Yourself

Draw a picture to show how you feel.

Show it to your parents or guardians.

Learn on Your Own

Find a library book on health.

Use Thinking Skills

Why should you have good character?

Be a Good Citizen

Tell two laws you follow.

Family and Social Health

Lesson 5
Your Family

Lesson 6
One, Two, a Friend for You

Lesson 7
How You Treat Others

PRACTICE
HEALTH STANDARD 6 | **Make Wise Decisions**

Your friend wants you to cross the street. The light is red.

1. **Tell what the choices are.** Cross the street. Wait until the light turns green.

2. **Ask questions before you choose.**

   • Is it healthful to cross the street?
   • Is it safe to cross the street?
   • Do I follow laws if I cross the street?
   • Do I show respect for others if I cross the street.
   • Do I follow family rules if I cross the street?
   • Do I show good character if I cross the street?

3. **Tell what the wise decision is.** Should you cross the street? Should you say no?

4. **Tell why.** Tell why you do not cross the street.

Lesson 5 Your Family

Life Skills

I will get along with my family.

I will share feelings about family changes.

What You Will Be Able to Do

Tell what to do if you have family changes.

Tell things you learn in a family.

Tell why you should follow family rules.

Tell ways to help at home.

Words You Will Learn

A **family** is people who belong together.

A **rule** is a guide to tell you how to act.

Family rules are rules your family makes.

Chores are small jobs.

What Is a Family?

A **family** is people who belong together.

Some families have mothers and fathers.

Some families have sisters and brothers.

A family might have a newborn baby.

There might be stepparents in a family.

Suppose your family changes in some way.

Talk to your parents or guardian.

Share your feelings about family changes.

What Do You Learn in a Family?

You learn from your family.

You learn about love.

You learn how to get along with others.

You learn how to be healthy and safe.

What Are Family Rules?

A **rule** is a guide to tell you how to act.

Family rules are rules your family makes.

Your parents or guardian make family rules.

You should follow family rules.

Family rules keep you healthy and safe.

Name some family rules you
must follow.

How Can I Help at Home?

Chores are small jobs.

Each person in a family can do chores.

You might sweep the floor.

You might take out the trash.

You might make your bed.

You might put away your toys.

You might set the table.

What chores do you do?

Activity

Make a Family Album

1. Make a family album.
2. Use colored paper for the cover.
3. Draw a picture of your family on the cover.
4. Use white paper for the pages.
5. Draw pictures of your family together.
6. Show your family working and playing.

Lesson 5 Review

Health Questions

1. What can you do if your family changes? **page 29**
2. What are three things you learn in a family? **page 30**
3. Why should you follow family rules? **page 31**
4. What are five chores you can do? **page 32**

Lesson 6 One, Two, a Friend for You

Life Skills

I will make wise decisions with friends.

I will help others take care of their health.

What You Will Be Able to Do

Tell things friends can do together.

Tell how friends can make wise decisions.

Words You Will Learn

A **friend** is someone you know and like.

A **wise decision** is the best choice.

What Is a Friend?

A **friend** is someone you know and like.

Friends can play together.

Friends can share feelings.

Friends can help each other with chores.

Friends can help each other make decisions.

How Can Friends Make Wise Decisions?

A **wise decision** is the best choice.

Friends can make wise decisions.

They can ask questions before they decide.

Will our decision be healthful?

Will our decision be safe?

Will our decision follow laws?

Will our decision show we respect others?

Will our decision follow our family rules?

Will our decision show we have good character?

Activity

Make a New Friend

1. Bring something to school to share.

2. You might bring a game or toy.

3. Share it with a child you do not know well.

4. Ask questions.

5. Learn two things about your classmate.

Lesson 6 Review

Health Questions

1. What are four things friends can do together?
   page 35

2. How can friends make wise decisions?
   page 36

Lesson 7 How You Treat Others

Life Skills

I will show respect for others.

I will work out conflict.

What You Will Be Able to Do

Tell ways to show respect for others.

Tell ways to work out conflict.

Words You Will Learn

Respect is thinking highly of someone.

A **conflict** is a disagreement.

What Is Respect?

Respect is thinking highly of someone.

You can show respect for others.

Treat others in kind ways.

Do not talk when someone is talking to you.

Take your turn when you and others are waiting.

Be fair when you play with others.

Answer when someone speaks to you.

Be fair when you play with others.

What Is Conflict?

A **conflict** is a disagreement.

You can work out conflict.

Stay calm.

Listen to the other person.

Tell your side.

Think of ways to work things out.

Agree on a healthful and safe way.

Activity
Say a Pledge Not to Fight

I will keep away from fights.
I will not punch, shove, kick, or bite.
Suppose someone wants to fight today.
I will talk it out or walk away.

Lesson 7 Review

Health Questions

1. What are ways to show respect for others?
page 39

2. What are ways to work out conflict? **page 40**

Health Questions

1. Why should you follow family rules?
   Lesson 5 page 31

2. How can friends make wise decisions?
   Lesson 6 page 36

3. What are ways to work out conflict?
   Lesson 7 page 40

Health Words

Write the answers on your paper.

family
friend
conflict

1. A _____ is a disagreement. **Lesson 7**

2. A _____ is people who belong together.
   Lesson 5

3. A _____ is someone you know and like.
   Lesson 6

Make Wise Decisions™

Your friend wants you to fight.

Suppose you fight.

- Is it safe?

- Do you follow family rules?

- Do you show good character?

What should you do?

Health Skills

Express Yourself

Draw a picture of something you do well.

Give it to an older family member.

Learn on Your Own

Find out what the word stepfamily means.

Use Thinking Skills

Why do loving parents make rules for children?

Be a Good Citizen

Help a family member do a chore.

Growth and Development

Help Others to Be Safe and Healthy

Practice this standard at the end of this unit.

1. **Choose a safe, healthful action.** Eat green leafy vegetables.

2. **Tell others about it.** Tell your classmates you eat vegetables. You eat lettuce. Tell them why.

3. **Do the safe, healthful action.** Tell when you would eat vegetables.

4. **Help others do the safe, healthful action.** Cut out a picture of a green, leafy vegetable from a magazine. Write: Eat your vegetables!

Lesson

8 I Love My Body Book

Life Skills

I will take care of my body.

I will choose habits to grow up healthy.

I will learn ways my body changes.

What You Will Be Able to Do

Tell ways to take care of body parts.

Words You Will Learn

Words you will learn are on the next page.

I Love My Body

The **heart** is a body part that pumps blood.

The **brain** is a body part that tells you what to do.

Lungs are body parts that help you get air.

The **stomach** is a body part that changes food.

Bones are hard body parts.

Muscles are body parts that help you move.

I Love My Bones

Bones are hard body parts.

Drink milk to make bones strong.

Exercise to make bones thick.

Play safely so you do not break bones.

I Love My Heart

The **heart** is a body part that pumps blood.

Smoking can harm your heart.

Do not smoke or breathe smoke.

Exercise to make your heart strong.

I Love My Stomach

The **stomach** is a body part that changes food.

Chew food before you swallow it.

Drink plenty of water.

Do not eat too many spicy foods.

I Love My Muscles

Muscles are body parts that help you move.

Exercise to make muscles strong.

Stretch muscles so they will not be sore.

Eat green, leafy vegetables.

I Love My Brain

The **brain** is a body part that tells you what to do.

Wear a safety belt when you ride in a car.

Wear a batter's helmet for baseball.

Wear a helmet when you skate or bike.

I Love My Lungs

Lungs are body parts that help you get air.

Exercise to keep your lungs healthy.

Do not smoke or breathe smoke.

Do not breathe glue.

Activity

I Love My Body Bulletin Board

1. Make a bulletin board with your class.

2. Cut a large heart out of red paper.

3. Write the name of a body part on it.

4. Tell a way to take care of this body part.

5. Pin your heart on the bulletin board.

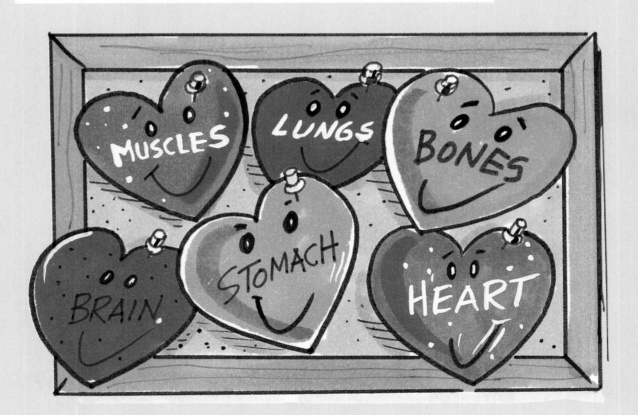

Lesson 8 Review

Health Questions

1. What are three ways to take care of your bones?
   page 48

2. What are two ways to take care of your heart?
   page 49

3. What are three ways to take care of your stomach?
   page 50

4. What are three ways to take care of your muscles?
   page 51

5. What are three ways to take care of your brain?
   page 52

6. What are three ways to take care of your lungs?
   page 53

Lesson

9 You Are Special

Life Skills

I will act in ways that show I am special.

I will work on ways to learn.

I will learn ways people age.

What You Will Be Able to Do

Tell ways you are special.

Tell ways to learn.

Tell ways you will age.

Words You Will Learn

To be **special** is to be very important.

To **learn** is to get to know something.

To **age** is to grow older.

How Am I Special?

To be **special** is to be very important.

You are special.

No one looks just like you do.

No one acts just like you do.

You are special to your family.

You are special to your friends.

My Health Plan

Use the same life skill.
Make your own Health Plan.

Work on Ways to Learn

 **Life Skill**

I will work on ways to learn.

Name_____

Date_____

My Plan: To **learn** is to get to know something.

These are two ways to learn.

- **I will read at home every day.**
- **I will tell my family a new word every day.**

Words I Learned:

Sunday To cooperate is to work together._____

Monday_____

Tuesday_____

Wednesday_____

Thursday_____

Friday_____

Saturday_____

How Will I Age?

To **age** is to grow older.

Your body will grow.

You will learn more.

Someday you will be a grown-up.

Lesson 9 Review

Health Questions

1. How are you special? **page 57**

2. What are two ways you can learn? **page 58**

3. What are two ways you will age? **page 59**

Unit 3 Review

Health Questions

1. What are two ways to take care of your heart?
   Lesson 8 page 49

2. What are three ways to take care of your brain?
   Lesson 8 page 52

3. How are you special? **Lesson 9 page 57**

4. What are two ways you can learn?
   Lesson 9 page 58

Health Words

Write the answers on your paper.

| heart |
| muscles |
| special |
| learn |

1. To be _____ is to be very important.
   Lesson 9

2. _____ are body parts that help you move.
   Lesson 8

3. To _____ is to get to know something.
   Lesson 9

4. The _____ is a body part that pumps blood.
   Lesson 8

Make Wise Decisions™

You forget to bring your helmet to the park.

Suppose you skate without a helmet.

- Is it safe?

- Do you follow family rules?

What should you do?

Health Skills

Express Yourself

Write three new words you know.

Learn on Your Own

Foods made with milk make bones strong.

Look at home for two foods made with milk.

Use Thinking Skills

Why do you need fresh air when you use glue?

Be a Good Citizen

Help a younger brother or sister learn.

Nutrition

Lesson 10
Steps to Good Eating

Lesson 11
Choose Healthful Foods

Lesson 12
Table Manners Please

PRACTICE

HEALTH STANDARD 2

Get What You Need for Good Health

Practice this standard at the end of this unit.

1. Tell what you need for good health.

Eat snacks low in sugar.

2. Find what you need for good health.

Read the facts in this book.

3. Check out what you need for good health.

Ask your parent to name healthful snacks.

4. Take action when something is not right.

Suppose someone gives you a cookie. Tell your parent you want a healthful snack.

Lesson 10
Steps to Good Eating

Life Skills

I will use the Food Guide Pyramid.

I will follow the Diet Guidelines.

I will read food labels.

What You Will Be Able to Do

Name the five healthful food groups.

Name the Diet Guidelines.

Tell what a food label shows.

Words You Will Learn

A **food group** is foods that are alike.

The **Food Guide Pyramid** shows the five food groups.

The **Diet Guidelines** are rules for eating.

Activity

Fill Up with Healthful Foods

1. Your teacher will cut out a paper person.

2. Your teacher will place it on the wall.

3. Look at old magazines.

4. Cut out pictures of two healthful foods.

5. Tape them to the paper person.

What Is the Food Guide Pyramid?

Healthful foods are in five food groups.

A **food group** is foods that are alike.

Look at the picture on the next page.

The **Food Guide Pyramid** shows the five food groups.

Eat foods from each food group every day.

Fats, Oils, and Sweets is not a food group.

Use small amounts of fats, oils, and sweets.

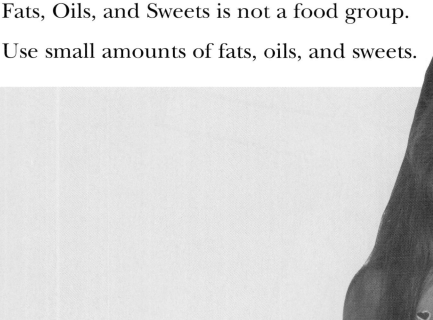

The Food Guide Pyramid

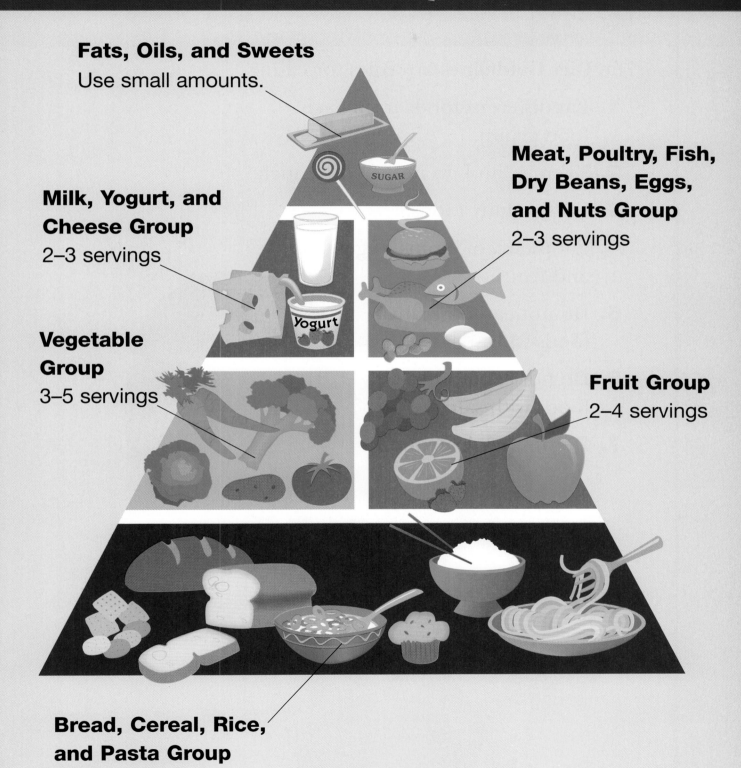

Fats, Oils, and Sweets
Use small amounts.

**Milk, Yogurt, and
Cheese Group**
2–3 servings

**Meat, Poultry, Fish,
Dry Beans, Eggs,
and Nuts Group**
2–3 servings

**Vegetable
Group**
3–5 servings

Fruit Group
2–4 servings

**Bread, Cereal, Rice,
and Pasta Group**
6–11 servings

What Are the Diet Guidelines?

The **Diet Guidelines** are rules for eating.

1. Eat different foods from each food group.

2. Exercise and do not eat too much.

3. Eat few fatty foods.

4. Eat plenty of grains, vegetables, and fruits.

5. Do not eat too many foods with sugar.

6. Do not eat too many foods with salt.

7. Do not drink alcohol.

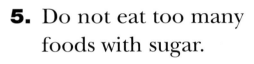

What Is a Food Label?

A food label shows facts about food.

It shows how much sugar is in a food.

It shows how much fat is in a food.

Sugars
A food label shows how much sugar is in the food.

Total Fat
A food label shows how much fat is in the food.

Food Label for Peanut Butter

Nutrition Facts

Serving Size 2 Tbsp. (35g)

Servings Per Container about 14

Calories 190

Fat Cal. 110

*Percent Daily Values (DV) are based on a 2,000 calorie diet.

Amount/Serving	%DV*	Amount/Serving	%DV*
Total Fat 12g	**18**%	**Total Carb.** 15g	**5**%
Sat Fat 2.5g	**12**%	Dietary Fiber 2g	**8**%
Cholest. 0mg	**0**%	Sugars 4g	
Sodium 220mg	**9**%	**Protein** 8g	

Iron 4% • Niacin 25% • Vitamin B₆ 6% • Folic Acid 6%

Magnesium 15% • Zinc 6% • Copper 10%

Not a significant source of vitamin A, vitamin C, and calcium.

Lesson 10 Review

Health Questions

1. What are the five healthful food groups? **page 67**

2. What are the seven Diet Guidelines? **page 68**

3. What are two things a food label shows? **page 69**

Lesson 11
Choose Healthful Foods

Life Skills

I will eat healthful meals and snacks.

I will choose healthful fast foods.

I will stay at a healthful weight.

What You Will Be Able to Do

Tell how to choose healthful snacks.

Tell how to choose healthful fast foods.

Tell how to stay at a healthful weight.

Words You Will Learn

A **snack** is food or drinks between meals.

A **fast food** is a food that is served fast.

Breakfast is the first meal of the day.

A **healthful weight** is the best weight for you.

What Are Healthful Snacks?

A **snack** is food or drinks between meals.

Eat snacks from the five food groups.

Eat snacks that are low in sugar.

Eat snacks that are low in fat.

Eat snacks that do not have caffeine.

Caffeine is found in soda pop and chocolate.

Caffeine makes you jumpy.

Fruit cocktail

Fat-free pretzel

Low-fat cereal

Strawberries

Carrot sticks

What Are Healthful Fast Foods?

A **fast food** is a food that is served fast.

You get fast foods at fast food restaurants.

Choose healthful fast foods.

Choose fast foods that are low in sugar.

Choose fast foods that are low in fat.

Burger on whole-wheat bun

Juice

Chicken taco

Veggie pizza

Activity

Eat a Healthful Breakfast

Breakfast is the first meal of the day.

Breakfast gives you energy in the morning.

1. Your teacher will make two big paper footprints.

2. Place your left foot on the left footprint.

3. Tell a breakfast food that gives you energy.

4. Place your right foot on the right footprint.

5. Tell a way you use energy in the morning.

You have a healthful weight when you get and use energy.

A **healthful weight** is the best weight for you.

Lesson 11 Review

Health Questions

1. How can you choose healthful snacks?
   page 71

2. How can you choose healthful fast foods?
   page 72

Lesson 12 Table Manners Please

Life Skills

I will protect myself from germs in food.

I will use good table manners.

What You Will Be Able to Do

Tell why you wash your hands before you eat.

Name good table manners.

Words You Will Learn

A **germ** is a tiny living thing.

Good table manners are nice ways to eat.

Why Should I Wash My Hands Before I Eat?

A **germ** is a tiny living thing.

Germs are on things you touch.

The germs get on your hands.

The germs get in your mouth when you eat.

You might get sick from the germs.

Wash your hands before you eat.

What Are Good Table Manners?

Good table manners are nice ways to eat.

Wash your hands before you eat.

Chew with your mouth closed.

Say, "Excuse me" if you burp.

Do not stuff your mouth full of food.

Activity
Manners at My Table

1. Get in a circle with your class.

2. Pass a spoon around the circle.

3. Say the rhyme with your class.

4. Someone will have the spoon on "bite."

5. That person tells a good table manner.

I invite you in to eat.

You come in and take your seat.

Name a way to be polite.

And I will let you have a bite.

Lesson 12 Review

Health Questions

1. Why wash your hands before you eat? **page 75**

2. What are four good table manners? **page 76**

Health Questions

1. What are the five healthful food groups?
Lesson 10 pages 66–67

2. What are the seven Diet Guidelines?
Lesson 10 page 68

3. How can you eat healthful snacks?
Lesson 11 page 71

4. Why wash your hands before you eat?
Lesson 12 page 75

5. What are four good table manners?
Lesson 12 page 76

Health Words

Write the answers on your paper.

| breakfast |
| Diet Guidelines |
| fast food |
| good table manners |

1. _____ is the first meal of the day. **Lesson 11**

2. A _____ _____ is a food that is served fast. **Lesson 11**

3. _____ _____ _____ are nice ways to eat. **Lesson 12**

4. The _____ _____ are rules for eating. **Lesson 10**

Make Wise Decisions™

You go to a fast food restaurant.

Suppose you order fries and a soda pop.

- Is it healthful?

- Do you show respect for others?

- Do you follow family rules?

What should you do?

Health Skills

Express Yourself

Draw a food from each food group.

Learn on Your Own

Find three snacks that are low in fat.

Use Thinking Skills

Why should you use good table manners?

Be a Good Citizen

Wash your hands before you set the table.

Personal Health and Physical Activity

Lesson 13
Sit and Stand Tall

Lesson 14
Exercise and Fitness

Lesson 15
Checkups

PRACTICE

HEALTH STANDARD 3

Make Health Plans

Practice this standard at the end of this unit.

1. Tell the life skill you will do.

I will be neat and clean.

2. Give a plan for what you will do.

Read page 84. Tell what you will do.

3. Keep track of what you do.

Write a list of things you do to be neat and clean.

Lesson 13 Sit and Stand Tall

Life Skills

I will get plenty of sleep and rest.

I will be neat and clean.

What You Will Be Able to Do

Tell how much sleep you need.

Tell how you can groom yourself.

Tell why you need good posture.

Words You Will Learn

Sleep is a time when you are not awake.

Grooming is making your body neat and clean.

Posture is the way you sit and stand.

My Health Plan

**Use the same life skill.
Make your own Health Plan.**

Get Plenty of Sleep

Life Skill — I will get plenty of sleep and rest.

Name_____

Date_____

My Plan: **Sleep** is a time when you are not awake.

- **I need about 11 hours of sleep each night.**
- **I need more sleep if I am sick.**
- **I need more sleep if I am very tired.**

What I Did:

Day	Time I Went to Bed	Time I Got Up
Sunday	8:00 pm	7:00 am
Monday		
Tuesday		
Wednesday		
Thursday		
Friday		
Saturday		

What Is Grooming?

Grooming is making your body neat and clean.

You can groom yourself.

Wash your hands with soap and water.

Take a bath each day.

Wash your hair.

Keep your nails clean and trimmed.

Wear clean clothes.

What Is Good Posture?

Posture is the way you sit and stand.

Do not slump.

Sit straight in a chair.

Stand straight when you walk.

Then body parts work right.

You look neat.

Lesson 13 Review

Health Questions

1. How many hours of sleep do you need?
page 83

2. How can you groom yourself? **page 84**

3. Why do you need good posture? **page 85**

Lesson 14 Exercise and Fitness

Life Skills

I will get plenty of exercise.

I will exercise in safe ways.

I will follow safety rules for sports and games.

What You Will Be Able to Do

Tell exercises to do to warm up.

Tell why you need fitness.

Tell how to work out to get heart fitness.

Words You Will Learn

To **exercise** is to move your muscles.

To **warm up** is to get muscles ready to move.

Fitness is being in top form from exercise.

Heart fitness is having a strong heart.

Activity

Start Your Workout with a Warm-Up

To **exercise** is to move your muscles.

Warm up before you do hard exercise.

To **warm up** is to get muscles ready to move.

1. Move like an animal to warm up.

2. Bend over and walk like an elephant.

3. Walk slowly like a turtle.

4. Run slowly like a bear.

Move like an animal to warm up.

What Is Fitness?

Fitness is being in top form from exercise.

Fitness helps you exercise for a long time.

Fitness keeps you from getting tired easily.

Fitness helps you have strong muscles.

Ride your bike
to have fitness.
Wear a helmet.
Wear knee and
elbow pads.
Follow safety rules.

My Health Plan

Use the same life skill. Make your own Health Plan.

Work Out to Get Heart Fitness

 **Life Skill**

I will get plenty of exercise.

Name _____

Date _____

My Plan: **Heart fitness** is having a strong heart.

- **Do exercises for heart fitness every day.**
- **Get your heart rate up.**
- **Exercise for 15 minutes or more.**

What I Did:

Sunday _I rode my bike for 15 minutes._

Monday _____

Tuesday _____

Wednesday _____

Thursday _____

Friday _____

Saturday _____

What Is The President's Challenge?

The President's Challenge is a fitness test.

It is for boys and girls ages 6 to 17.

There are five parts.

Curl-Ups show if muscles below the stomach are strong.

The **Shuttle Run** shows if leg muscles are strong.

It shows if you have heart fitness.

The **One-Mile Walk or Run** shows if leg muscles are strong.

It shows if you have heart fitness.

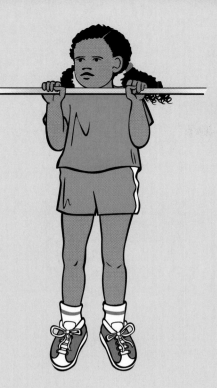

Pull-Ups show if arm and shoulder muscles are strong.

The **V-Sit and Reach** shows if leg muscles stretch easily.

It shows if back muscles stretch easily.

Lesson 14 Review

Health Questions

1. What are exercises to do to warm up?
   page 87

2. Why do you need fitness? **page 88**

3. How can you work out to get heart fitness?
   page 89

Lesson 15 Checkups

Life Skills

I will have checkups.

I will keep a health record.

I will take care of my teeth.

What You Will Be Able to Do

Tell what happens in a checkup.

Tell what happens in a dental checkup.

Tell what flossing is.

Tell six ways to care for teeth.

Words You Will Learn

A **checkup** is a check to see how healthy you are.

A **cavity** is a hole in a tooth.

Flossing is removing food stuck between teeth.

What Is a Checkup?

A **checkup** is a check to see how healthy you are.

You write what you do for health in a health record.

You bring your health record to the doctor.

Your doctor asks you what you do.

Then the doctor checks your body.

The doctor checks to see how you grow.

The doctor listens to your heart.

The doctor checks your ears and eyes.

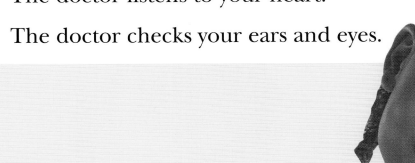

What Is a Dental Checkup?

A dentist checks your teeth.

A dentist can tell how new teeth are growing.

Suppose you have a cavity.

A **cavity** is a hole in a tooth.

Your dentist might give you a filling.

A filling fills the hole in the tooth.

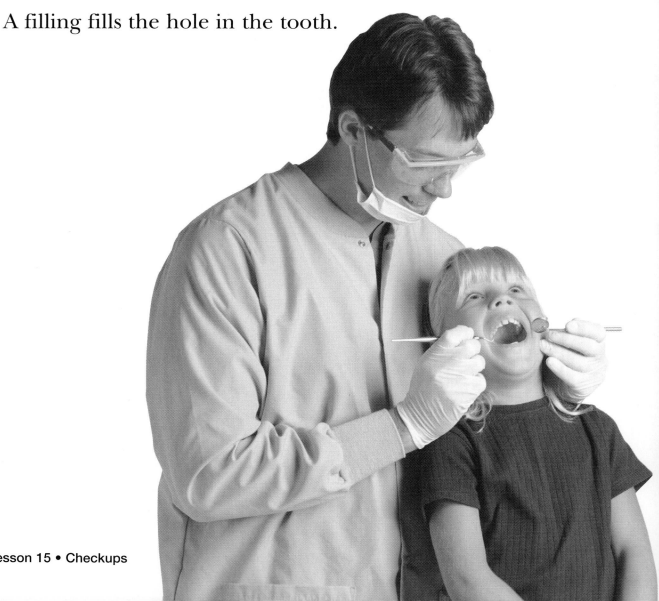

A dental hygienist works with a dentist.

This health helper cleans your teeth.

This health helper takes X-rays.

X-rays are pictures of teeth.

Cooperate with this health helper.

Brush your teeth after every meal.

How to Brush Your Teeth

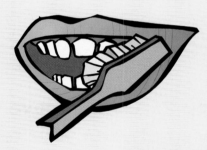

Brush the outside of the teeth.

Brush the inside of the teeth.

Brush the gums and tongue.

What Is Flossing?

Flossing is removing food stuck between teeth.

Flossing removes germs, too.

Floss every day.

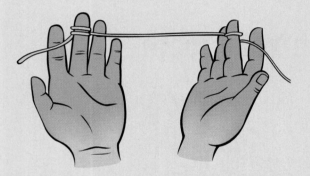

Step 1: Wind the floss around your middle fingers.

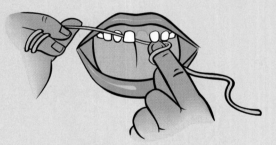

Step 2: Gently move the floss between your teeth.

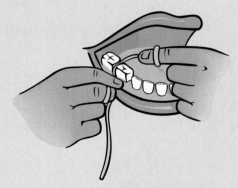

Step 3: Move the floss upward on the bottom teeth. Move the floss downward on the top teeth.

Activity
Ways to Care for Teeth

1. Make six big cards like the ones below.

2. Pair up with a partner.

3. Put both sets of cards face down.

4. Take turns turning them over to get a match.

Floss every day.	Drink milk.	Brush after meals.	Get dental checkups.	Do not bite hard candy.	Wear a safety belt in a car.

Lesson 15 Review

Health Questions

1. What happens in a checkup? **page 93**

2. What happens in a dental checkup? **page 94**

3. What is flossing? **page 96**

4. What are six ways to care for teeth? **page 97**

Unit 5 Review

Health Questions

1. How many hours of sleep do you need?
Lesson 13 page 83

2. Why do you need fitness? **Lesson 14 page 88**

3. How can you work out to get heart fitness?
Lesson 14 page 89

4. What are six ways to care for teeth?
Lesson 15 page 97

Health Words

Write the answers on your paper.

grooming

posture

heart fitness

cavity

1. _____ _____ is having a strong heart.
Lesson 14

2. A _____ is a hole in a tooth. **Lesson 15**

3. _____ is the way you sit and stand.
Lesson 13

4. _____ is making your body neat and clean. **Lesson 13**

Make Wise Decisions™

You cannot get the cap off a bottle.

Suppose you use your teeth to get it off.

- Is it healthful to use your teeth?
- Is it safe to use your teeth?

What should you do?

Health Skills

Express Yourself

Find a magazine with pictures.

Cut out pictures of grooming products.

Paste them on poster board.

Learn on Your Own

Talk to your dentist about toothbrushes.

Learn the best one for you.

Use Thinking Skills

Why do you need to bathe or shower every day?

Be a Good Citizen

Take a walk with a family member.

Say NO!

Alcohol, Tobacco, and Other Drugs

PRACTICE

HEALTH STANDARD 5

Work Out Conflict

Practice this standard at the end of this unit.

Suppose a friend gives you medicine to try. You do not want it. You are upset.

1. **Stay calm.** Tell how you can stay calm.

2. **Listen to the other person.** What is this person trying to get you to do?

3. **Tell your side.** Say, "It is not safe to take medicine from a friend."

4. **Think of ways to work things out.** Tell your friend it is wrong. Tell an adult about your friend.

5. **Agree on a healthful and safe way.** Tell your friend to return the medicine.

Lesson 16 Be Wise About Medicine

Life Skill

I will use medicine in safe ways.

What You Will Be Able to Do

Tell what medicine does.

Tell rules for safe use of medicine.

Words You Will Learn

A **drug** is something that changes how the mind or body works.

Medicine is a drug that helps the mind or body.

What Is Medicine?

A **drug** is something that changes how the mind or body works.

Medicine is a drug that helps the mind or body.

Some medicine kills germs that make you sick.

You might take medicine for a sore throat.

Some medicine kills germs that get in cuts.

Some children have special health needs.

They might need medicine every day.

What Is the Safe Use of Medicine?

Take medicine only from certain grown-ups.

Take it from your parents or guardian.

Take it from a doctor or nurse.

Take only your own medicine.

Keep medicine in a safe place.

Make Wise Decisions™

You have a sore throat.

Suppose you take your brother's medicine.

1. Is it healthful?

2. Do you follow laws?

3. Do you follow family rules?

What should you do?

Lesson 16 Review

Health Questions

1. What does medicine do? **page 103**

2. What is the safe use of medicine? **page 104**

Lesson 17 Alcohol Harms Health

Life Skill

I will not drink alcohol.

What You Will Be Able to Do

Tell how alcohol harms health.

Tell how to say NO to drinking.

Words You Will Learn

Alcohol is a drug found in some drinks.

Say NO skills are ways to say NO.

What Is Alcohol?

Alcohol is a drug found in some drinks.

It is found in beer and wine.

It can harm the heart and brain.

It causes the brain to slow down.

It causes a person to make wrong decisions.

It causes the body to slow down.

It causes a person to have accidents.

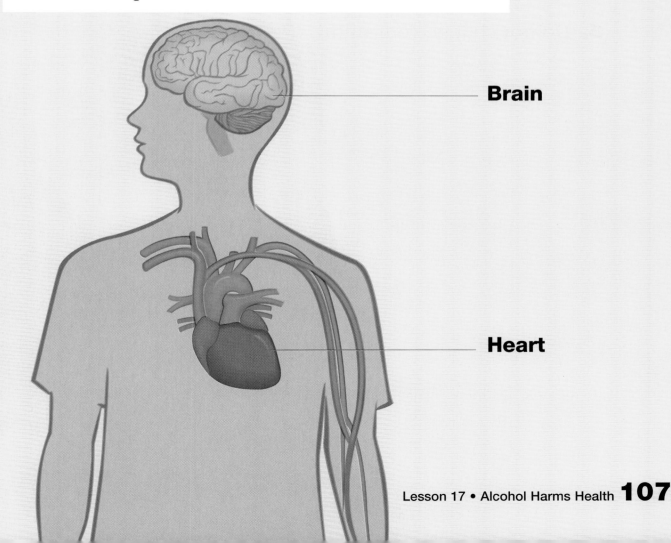

Brain

Heart

How Can I Say NO to Alcohol?

Suppose someone asks you to drink alcohol.

Use say NO skills.

Say NO skills are ways to say NO.

1. Look at the person.
2. Say, "NO, I will not drink alcohol."
3. Tell the bad results of alcohol.
4. Say NO again if you need to.
5. Do not change your mind.

Activity

Say NO to Alcohol Pledge

Say this pledge with your class.

I say NO to alcohol.
I do not want to trip and fall.
I do not want to fail in school.
Alcohol is never cool.

Lesson 17 Review

Health Questions

1. How can alcohol harm health? **page 107**

2. How can you say NO to alcohol? **page 108**

Lesson 18 Tobacco Harms Health

Life Skills

I will not use tobacco.

I will stay away from secondhand smoke.

I will tell ways people who use harmful drugs can get help.

What You Will Be Able to Do

Tell why tobacco is harmful.

Tell groups that help people stop using tobacco.

Tell why secondhand smoke is harmful.

Words You Will Learn

Tobacco is a plant that has a harmful drug.

Secondhand smoke is smoke from other people's cigarettes and cigars.

Smokeless tobacco is tobacco for chewing.

Why Is Tobacco Harmful?

Tobacco is a plant that has a harmful drug.

Cigarettes and cigars are made from tobacco.

Smokeless tobacco is tobacco for chewing.

The drug in tobacco harms your heart.

You can get hooked on this drug.

Hooked means you use it again and again.

Smoking cigarettes and cigars harms lungs.

Chewing tobacco can cause teeth to fall out.

People hooked on tobacco need help.

The American Cancer Society helps.

The American Heart Association helps.

The American Lung Association helps.

What Is Secondhand Smoke?

Secondhand smoke is smoke from other people's cigarettes and cigars.

It harms your heart and lungs.

It makes you cough.

It makes your eyes water.

Suppose someone smokes around you.

Ask the person to stop.

Try not to be around someone who smokes.

GASP

Activity

Stomp Out Smoking

1. Look at old magazines.

2. Cut out an ad for cigarettes.

3. An ad is a message to get you to buy something.

4. Place the ad on the floor.

5. Stomp on the ad.

6. Say, "I will not use tobacco."

Lesson 18 Review

Health Questions

1. Why is tobacco harmful? **page 111**

2. What three groups help people stop using tobacco? **page 111**

3. What is secondhand smoke? **page 112**

Lesson 19 Drug-Free Me

Life Skill
I will not use drugs that are against the law.

What You Will Be Able to Do

Tell what drug-free is.

Tell drugs that are against the law.

Words You Will Learn

To be **drug-free** is not to use harmful drugs.

A **law** is a rule that keeps people safe.

What Is Drug-Free?

To be **drug-free** is not to use harmful drugs.

Do not try a drug.

Say NO if someone tries to give you a drug.

Do not have friends who use drugs.

Do not go places where people use drugs.

I will not use drugs that are against the law.

What Drugs Are Against the Law?

A **law** is a rule that keeps people safe.

People can go to jail if they break a law.

It is against the law to use some drugs.

Marijuana is a drug that is against the law.

Cocaine is a drug that is against the law.

Crack is a drug that is against the law.

Activity

Don't Break the Law

1. Make a police officer's hat.

2. Put the hat on your head.

3. Say, "I don't break the law."

4. Say, "I am drug-free."

5. Then tell one way to be drug-free.

Lesson 19 Review

Health Questions

1. What is drug-free? **page 115**

2. What drugs are against the law? **page 116**

Unit 6 Review

Health Questions

1. What does medicine do? **Lesson 16 page 103**

2. How can you say NO to alcohol? **Lesson 17 page 108**

3. Why is tobacco harmful? **Lesson 18 page 111**

4. What is secondhand smoke? **Lesson 18 page 112**

5. What is drug-free? **Lesson 19 page 115**

Health Words

Write the answers on your paper.

alcohol
drug
law
tobacco
smokeless tobacco

1. _____ is a plant that has a harmful drug. **Lesson 18**

2. A _____ is something that changes how the mind or body works. **Lesson 16**

3. A _____ is a rule that keeps people safe. **Lesson 19**

4. _____ is a drug found in some drinks. **Lesson 17**

5. _____ _____ is tobacco for chewing. **Lesson 18**

Make Wise Decisions™

A friend dares you to chew tobacco.

Suppose you chew tobacco.

- Is it healthful?

- Do you follow laws?

- Do you follow family rules?

What should you do?

Health Skills

Express Yourself

Practice say NO skills with friends.

Learn on Your Own

What is the harmful drug in tobacco called?

Use Thinking Skills

What grown-ups can give you medicine?

Be a Good Citizen

Look for pictures of healthful drinks.

Share them with friends.

Communicable and Chronic Diseases

Lesson 20
Don't Spread Germs
Lesson 21
When You Are Sick
Lesson 22
Stop Heart Disease
Lesson 23
Wear Sunscreen

PRACTICE

HEALTH STANDARD 1

Learn Health Facts

Practice this standard at the end of this unit.

1. **Study and learn health facts.**

   Tell three exercises you can do.

2. **Ask questions about health facts.**

   What body part do these exercises help?

3. **Answer questions about health facts.**

   Ask your parent about exercises for the heart.

4. **Use health facts to do life skills.**

   What exercise can you do at home?

Lesson 20 Don't Spread Germs

Life Skill

I will protect myself and others from germs.

What You Will Be Able to Do

Tell how germs are spread.

Tell when to wash your hands.

Tell what a vaccine is.

Words You Will Learn

A **germ** is a tiny living thing.

A **vaccine** is medicine that keeps germs from harming you.

How Do Germs Spread?

A **germ** is a tiny living thing.

Germs are so small you cannot see them.

Germs can spread.

You can breathe germs in the air.

You can drink germs in dirty water.

You can get germs from objects you touch.

Germs can make you ill.

My Health Plan

**Use the same life skill.
Make your own Health Plan.**

Wash My Hands

I will protect myself and others from germs.

Name _____

Date _____

My Plan: Here are two times I will wash my hands.

- **I will wash my hands before I eat.**
- **I will wash my hands after I use the restroom.**

What I Did:

	S	M	T	W	Th	F	S
Washed hands before eating	✓	✓	✓	✓	✓	✓	✓
Washed hands after using the restroom	✓	✓	✓	✓	✓	✓	✓

What Is a Vaccine?

A **vaccine** is medicine that keeps germs from harming you.

You get a vaccine to keep away measles.

You get a vaccine to keep away chickenpox.

You might get a vaccine in a shot.

Lesson 20 Review

Health Questions

1. What are three ways germs can spread? **page 123**

2. When should you wash your hands? **page 124**

3. What is a vaccine? **page 125**

Lesson
21 When You Are Sick

Life Skills

I will learn symptoms and treatment for diseases.

I will tell ways to care for asthma.

I will tell ways to care for allergies.

What You Will Be Able to Do

Tell what to do for a cold and a sore throat.

Tell what asthma is.

Tell what an allergy is.

Words You Will Learn

Asthma makes it hard to breathe sometimes.

An **allergy** is the body's bad reaction to something.

What Can I Do for a Cold and a Sore Throat?

A cold is caused by germs.

Suppose you have a cold.

Get rest and sleep.

Drink plenty of water and juice.

A sore throat is caused by germs.

Suppose you have a sore throat.

Take medicine your doctor gives you.

Activity

Learn About Asthma

Asthma makes it hard to breathe sometimes.

What might it be like to have asthma?

1. Put a straw in your mouth.
2. Hold your nose.
3. Breathe through the straw.
4. Notice that it is easy to breathe.
5. Take the straw out of your mouth.
6. Put a coffee stirrer in your mouth.
7. Breathe through the coffee stirrer.
8. Notice that it is hard to breathe.

This is what it is like to have asthma.

Do NOT do this if you have asthma!

What Is an Allergy?

Some children have an allergy.

An **allergy** is the body's bad reaction to something.

You might have an allergy to grass.

Grass makes you cough and sneeze.

You might have an allergy to cats.

You might have trouble breathing around cats.

Lesson 21 Review

Health Questions

1. What can you do for a cold and a sore throat? **page 127**

2. What is asthma? **page 128**

3. What is an allergy? **page 129**

Lesson 22 Stop Heart Disease

Life Skill

I will choose habits that prevent heart disease.

What You Will Be Able to Do

Tell foods that help stop heart disease.

Tell exercises that help stop heart disease.

Words You Will Learn

Heart disease is a problem with how the heart works.

To **exercise** is to move your muscles.

What Foods Help Stop Heart Disease?

Blood vessels carry blood to the heart.

Suppose you eat a lot of fatty foods.

Fats from fatty foods stick to blood vessels.

There is less space in the blood vessels.

Then your heart does not get enough blood.

Heart disease is a problem with how the heart works.

Eat foods that keep your heart healthy.

Eat foods that are low in fat.

Eat fruits and vegetables.

Eat foods made of grains, like bread.

What Exercises Help Stop Heart Disease?

To **exercise** is to move your muscles.

Exercise can help stop heart disease.

Exercise can make your heart strong.

You can play and exercise at the same time.

Playing tag makes your heart strong.

Riding your bike makes your heart strong.

Tap dancing makes your heart strong.

Activity

"No Smoking" Heart

Smoking causes heart disease.

1. Draw and cut out a big heart.

2. Write "No Smoking" on the heart.

3. Put your heart on the bulletin board.

Lesson 22 Review

Health Questions

1. What foods help stop heart disease? **page 131**

2. What exercises help stop heart disease? **page 132**

Lesson 23 Wear Sunscreen

Life Skill

I will choose habits that prevent cancer.

What You Will Be Able to Do

Tell how to help stop cancer.

Tell how to protect yourself from the sun.

Words You Will Learn

Cancer is an illness in which harmful cells grow.

A **sunscreen** is a lotion that blocks the sun's rays.

What Is Cancer?

Cancer is an illness in which harmful cells grow.

You can help stop cancer.

Eat fruits and vegetables.

Do not smoke or chew tobacco.

Do not breathe secondhand smoke.

Protect yourself from the sun.

How Can I Protect Myself from the Sun?

The sun's rays can cause skin cancer.

Protect yourself from the sun's rays.

Do not be in the sun during certain times.

Stay out of the sun between 10:00 a.m. and 4:00 p.m.

Wear a hat.

Wear a sunscreen.

A **sunscreen** is a lotion that blocks the sun's rays.

Activity
"No Smoking" Pledge

Smoking can cause cancer.

1. Make up a pledge not to smoke.

2. Learn the pledge.

3. Say it with your friends.

Lesson 23 Review

Health Questions

1. How can you help stop cancer? **page 135**

2. How can you protect yourself from the sun?
   page 136

Unit 7 Review

Health Questions

1. When should you wash your hands? **Lesson 20 page 124**

2. What is a vaccine? **Lesson 20 page 125**

3. What is asthma? **Lesson 21 page 128**

4. What are exercises that help stop heart disease? **Lesson 22 page 132**

5. How can you help stop cancer? **Lesson 23 page 135**

Health Words

Write the answers on your paper.

allergy
germ
heart disease
sunscreen
vaccine

1. A _____ is a tiny living thing. **Lesson 20**

2. _____ _____ is a problem with how the heart works. **Lesson 22**

3. An _____ is the body's bad reaction to something. **Lesson 21**

4. A _____ is a lotion that blocks the sun's rays. **Lesson 23**

5. A _____ is medicine that keeps germs from harming you. **Lesson 20**

Make Wise Decisions™

Suppose you watch TV for hours every day.

You do not play and make your heart strong.

- Is it healthful?

- Do you follow family guidelines?

What should you do?

Health Skills

Express Yourself

Make a hat out of paper.

Write a way to protect yourself from the sun.

Learn on Your Own

Find out three vaccines you have had.

Use Thinking Skills

Why should you wear sunscreen in the sun?

Be a Good Citizen

Exercise with your family.

Consumer and Community Health

Lesson 24
Health Helpers

Lesson 25
Ads You See and Hear

Lesson 26
When You Shop

PRACTICE

HEALTH STANDARD 2

Get What You Need for Good Health

Practice this standard at the end of this unit.

1. Tell what you need for good health.

Find the word "dentist" on page 145.

2. Find what you need for good health.

Tell what a dentist does.

3. Check out what you need for good health.

Ask your parent where you can find a dentist.

4. Take action when something is not right.

Suppose you have a toothache. Tell how to get help.

Lesson 24 Health Helpers

Life Skills

I will cooperate with health helpers.

I will check out jobs in health.

What You Will Be Able to Do

Tell how health helpers help you.

Give examples of health helpers.

Words You Will Learn

A **health helper** helps you stay healthy.

To **cooperate** is to work together.

How Do Health Helpers Help You?

A **health helper** helps you stay healthy.

A health helper treats you when you are ill.

A health helper keeps you from getting sick.

A health helper helps you grow as you should.

You need to cooperate with health helpers.

To **cooperate** is to work together.

A teacher is a health helper.

Activity

Learn About a Job in Health

1. Read the boxes below.

2. Choose a health helper.

3. Tell the class a clue about a health helper.

4. Your classmates cannot look at their books.

5. Have the class guess the health helper.

Doctor

A doctor treats you if you are ill or hurt.

A doctor gives you medicine.

A doctor gives you a checkup.

Dentist

A dentist looks at X-rays of your teeth.

A dentist fills cavities.

A dentist tells you if you need braces.

Dental Hygienist

A dental hygienist works with a dentist.

A dental hygienist cleans your teeth.

A dental hygienist takes X-rays of your teeth.

Nurse

A nurse works with a doctor.

A nurse checks your height and weight.

A nurse gives first aid if you are hurt.

Lesson 24 Review

Health Questions

1. How do health helpers help you? **page 143**

2. Who are four health helpers? **pages 144–145**

Lesson 25

Ads You See and Hear

Life Skills

I will check out ads.

I will choose safe and healthful products.

I will check out ways to learn health facts.

What You Will Be Able to Do

Tell what an ad is.

Tell how to use a computer to find health facts.

Name healthful products.

Words You Will Learn

An **ad** is a message to get you to buy something.

A **health fact** is a true message about health.

What Is an Ad?

An **ad** is a message to get you to buy something.

You see ads on TV.

You hear ads on the radio.

Some ads have funny characters.

Some ads have cool music.

Ads try to get you to buy something.

Ask your parents or guardian before you buy.

What Are Healthful Products?

Your family buys healthful products.

A healthful product is something you use for health.

Toothpaste is a healthful product.

A bicycle is a healthful product.

Low-fat cereal is a healthful product.

Activity

Use Technology to Find Health Facts

1. Ask your parents or guardian first.

2. Use a computer.

3. Find the Web site www.epa.gov/kids/.

4. Copy two health facts.

A **health fact** is a true message about health.

Lesson 25 Review

Health Questions

1. What is an ad? **page 147**

2. What are three healthful products? **page 148**

3. How can you use a computer to find health facts? **page 149**

Lesson 26 When You Shop

Life Skills

I will make wise choices about time and money.

I will choose healthful entertainment.

What You Will Be Able to Do

Tell what to ask before you buy.

Tell how to manage your time.

Tell what healthful entertainment is.

Words You Will Learn

Entertainment is what you like to see and do.

Healthful entertainment is entertainment that keeps your mind and body healthy.

What Should I Ask Before I Buy?

Suppose you want to buy a game.

Ask two questions before you buy it.

Do I need it?

Suppose you have a lot of games.

Save your money for something you need.

Is it healthful and safe?

Suppose the game is for someone older.

Suppose the game is not safe.

Do not buy the game.

My Health Plan

Use the same life skill. Make your own Health Plan.

Manage My Time

Life Skill **I will make wise choices about time and money.**

Name ____________________

Date ____________________

My Plan: Here are ways I can plan my time.

- **I will study at the same time every day.**
- **I will clean my room so I can find things.**
- **I will watch TV for no more than one hour.**

I will put a check when I make a wise choice about time.

What I Did:

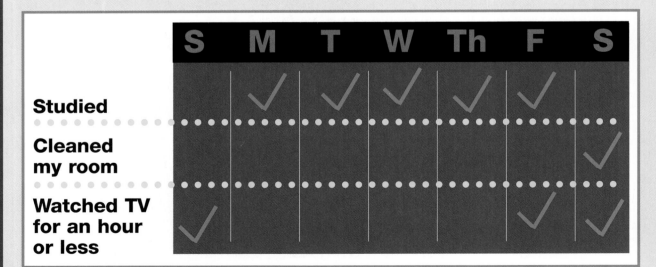

	S	M	T	W	Th	F	S
Studied		✓	✓	✓	✓	✓	
Cleaned my room							✓
Watched TV for an hour or less	✓					✓	✓

What Is Healthful Entertainment?

Entertainment is what you like to see and do.

Entertainment is TV and movies.

Entertainment is computer games.

Healthful entertainment is entertainment that keeps your mind and body healthy.

It follows your family's rules.

It shows people who have good character.

It does not show violence.

It does not show people saying bad words.

Lesson 26 Review

Health Questions

1. What should you ask before you buy? **page 151**

2. How can you plan your time? **page 152**

3. What is healthful entertainment? **page 153**

Unit 8 Review

Health Questions

1. Who are four health helpers? **Lesson 24 pages 144–145**

2. What is an ad? **Lesson 25 page 147**

3. What are three healthful products? **Lesson 25 page 148**

4. What should you ask before you buy? **Lesson 26 page 151**

5. What is healthful entertainment? **Lesson 26 page 153**

Health Words

Write the answers on your paper.

ad
cooperate
entertainment
health fact
health helper

1. _____ is what you like to see and do. **Lesson 26**

2. A _____ _____ helps you stay healthy. **Lesson 24**

3. An _____ is a message to get you to buy something. **Lesson 25**

4. To _____ is to work together. **Lesson 24**

5. A _____ _____ is a true message about health. **Lesson 25**

Make Wise Decisions™

A show that has bad language comes on TV.

Suppose you watch the show.

- Is it healthful?

- Do you follow family rules?

What should you do?

Health Skills

Express Yourself

Make up an ad for a healthful product.

Learn on Your Own

Some doctors take care of children only.

Find out what they are called.

Use Thinking Skills

What do you like about your favorite ad?

Be a Good Citizen

Talk to your dentist.

Ask which toothpaste is best for your family.

Unit 9

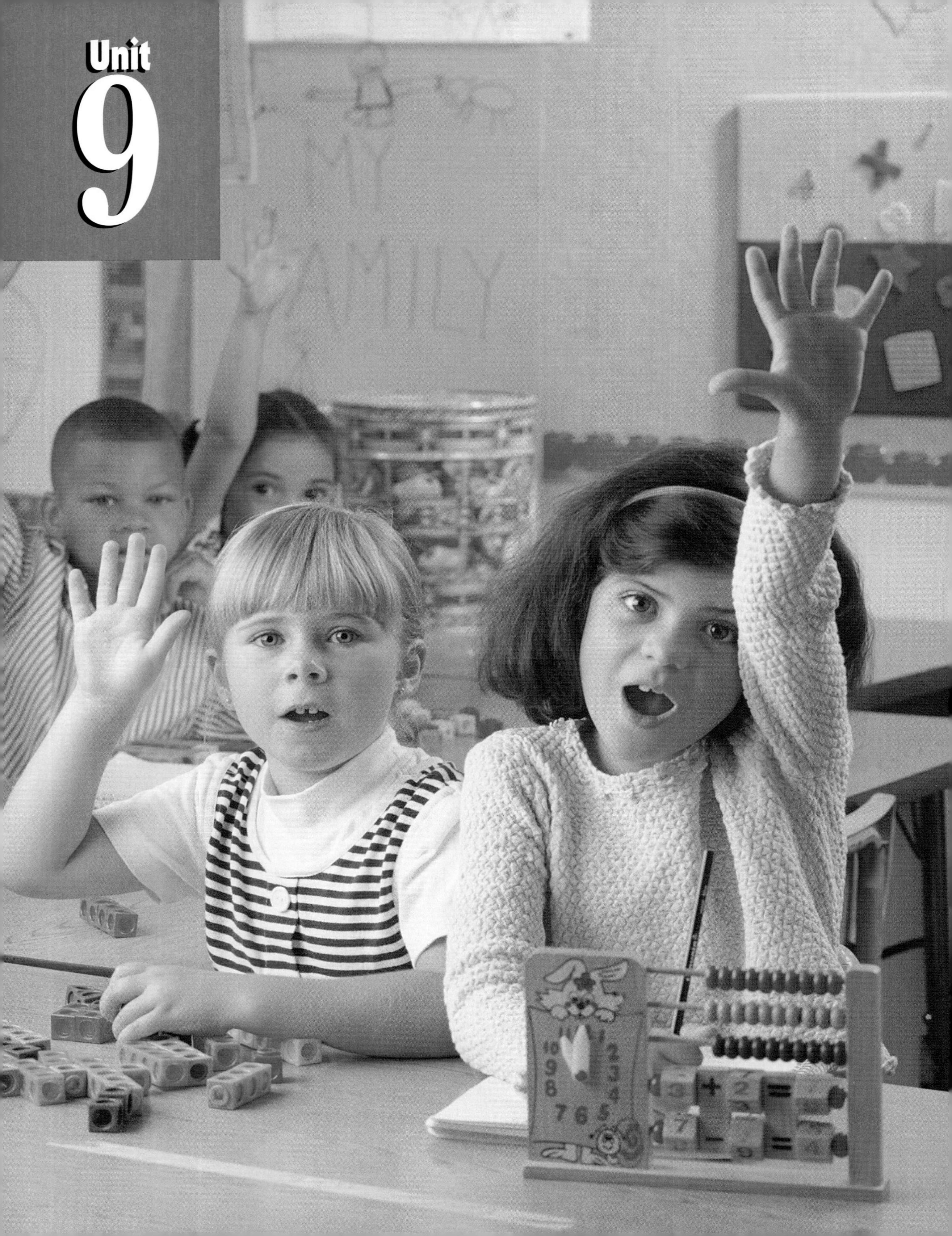

Environmental Health

Lesson 27
Turn It Off—Turn It Down
Lesson 28
Don't Make a Mess
Lesson 29
Warm Fuzzies

Help Others to be Safe and Healthy

Practice this standard at the end of this unit.

1. Choose a safe, healthful action.

I will not litter.

2. Tell others about it.

Tell your friends why they should not litter.

3. Do the safe, healthful action.

Throw trash away in a trash can.

4. Help others do the safe, healthful action.

Show others where they can throw away their trash.

Lesson

27 Turn It Off— Turn It Down

Life Skill

I will keep noise down.

What You Will Be Able to Do

Tell how you can keep noise down.

Tell why you need quiet time.

Words You Will Learn

Noise is sound that can harm you.

Quiet time is time you spend without noise.

What Is Noise?

Noise is sound that can harm you.

Noise can make it hard for you to think.

Loud noise can harm your hearing.

Do not play your radio or CD player loud.

Do not turn the sound way up on the TV.

Wear special ear muffs around loud noises.

Why Do I Need Quiet Time?

Quiet time is time you spend without noise.

Quiet time helps you think.

You think about things you have done.

You think about feelings you have.

Quiet time helps you study.

You pay attention to what you read.

Quiet time helps you slow down.

You give your body a chance to rest.

Make Wise Decisions™

You are listening to the radio.

Your brother tells you to play it louder.

Suppose you turn the sound way up.

1. Is it healthful?

2. Do you show respect for others?

3. Do you follow family rules?

What should you do?

Lesson 27 Review

Health Questions

1. How can you keep noise down? **page 159**

2. Why do you need quiet time? **page 160**

Lesson

28 Don't Make a Mess

Life Skills

I will help keep my environment clean.

I will help stop pollution.

I will not waste energy and resources.

What You Will Be Able to Do

Tell how litter harms land and water.

Tell how to keep the land clean.

Tell how to save water.

Words You Will Learn

Pollution is anything that harms the air, water, or land.

Litter is trash on the ground or in water.

What Is Pollution?

Pollution is anything that harms the air, water, or land.

One kind of pollution is litter.

Litter is trash on the ground or in water.

It is against the law to litter.

Litter makes the ground or water dirty.

Litter can have germs that make you sick.

Litter such as broken glass can cut you.

Throw litter in a trash can.

My Health Plan

Use the same life skill. Make your own Health Plan.

Do Not Litter

 **Life Skill**

I will help keep my environment clean.

Name _____

Date _____

My Plan: This is a way to keep the land clean.

- **I will throw litter in trash cans.**

I will make a check when I throw away litter.

What I Did:

Threw Away Litter

S	M	T	W	Th	F	S
✓	✓	✓	✓	✓	✓	✓

How Can I Save Water?

Do not use more water than you need.

Turn off the water when you brush your teeth.

Turn off the water after you wash your hands.

Take a shower instead of a bath.

**You need water.
Do not waste it.**

Lesson 28 Review

Health Questions

1. How does litter harm land and water? **page 163**

2. How can you keep the land clean? **page 164**

3. How can you save water? **page 165**

Lesson 29 Warm Fuzzies

Life Skill

I will help keep my environment friendly.

What You Will Be Able to Do

Tell how you can be friendly.

Tell how you can be a good neighbor.

Words You Will Learn

A **warm fuzzy** is a nice thing to say or do.

A **neighbor** is someone who lives near you.

How Can I Be Friendly?

A **warm fuzzy** is a nice thing to say or do.

You are friendly when you give a warm fuzzy.

Tell someone, "I'm glad you're my friend."

Say, "Thank you," when someone helps you.

Help someone who drops something.

Ask someone to play with you.

How Can I Be a Good Neighbor?

A **neighbor** is someone who lives near you.

You can be a good neighbor.

Wave and say, "Hello," to your neighbors.

Pick up trash around your neighborhood.

Do not let your dog bark late at night.

Activity

Give a Warm Fuzzy

1. Imagine what a warm fuzzy looks like.

2. Draw a picture and cut it out.

3. Give the warm fuzzy to a classmate.

4. Say something nice to your classmate.

Lesson 29 Review

Health Questions

1. How can you be friendly? **page 167**

2. How can you be a good neighbor? **page 168**

Health Questions

1. How can you keep noise down?
   Lesson 27 page 159

2. How does litter harm land and water?
   Lesson 28 page 163

3. How can you save water?
   Lesson 28 page 165

4. How can you be friendly?
   Lesson 29 page 167

5. How can you be a good neighbor?
   Lesson 29 page 168

Health Words

litter

neighbor

noise

quiet time

warm fuzzy

Write the answers on your paper.

1. _____ is trash on the ground or in water.
   Lesson 28

2. _____ _____ is time you spend without noise.
   Lesson 27

3. A _____ is someone who lives near you.
   Lesson 29

4. A _____ _____ is a nice thing to say or do.
   Lesson 29

5. _____ is sound that can harm you. **Lesson 27**

Make Wise Decisions™

You drop your box of juice by accident.

Suppose you leave the box on the ground.

- Is it healthful?

- Do you follow laws?

- Do you show respect for others?

What should you do?

Health Skills

Express Yourself

Put a picture of an ear by your TV.

Remember to keep the sound low on the TV.

Learn on Your Own

Find out one more way to save water.

Use Thinking Skills

What is a noise that might harm your ears?

Be a Good Citizen

Give a warm fuzzy to a neighbor.

Unit 10

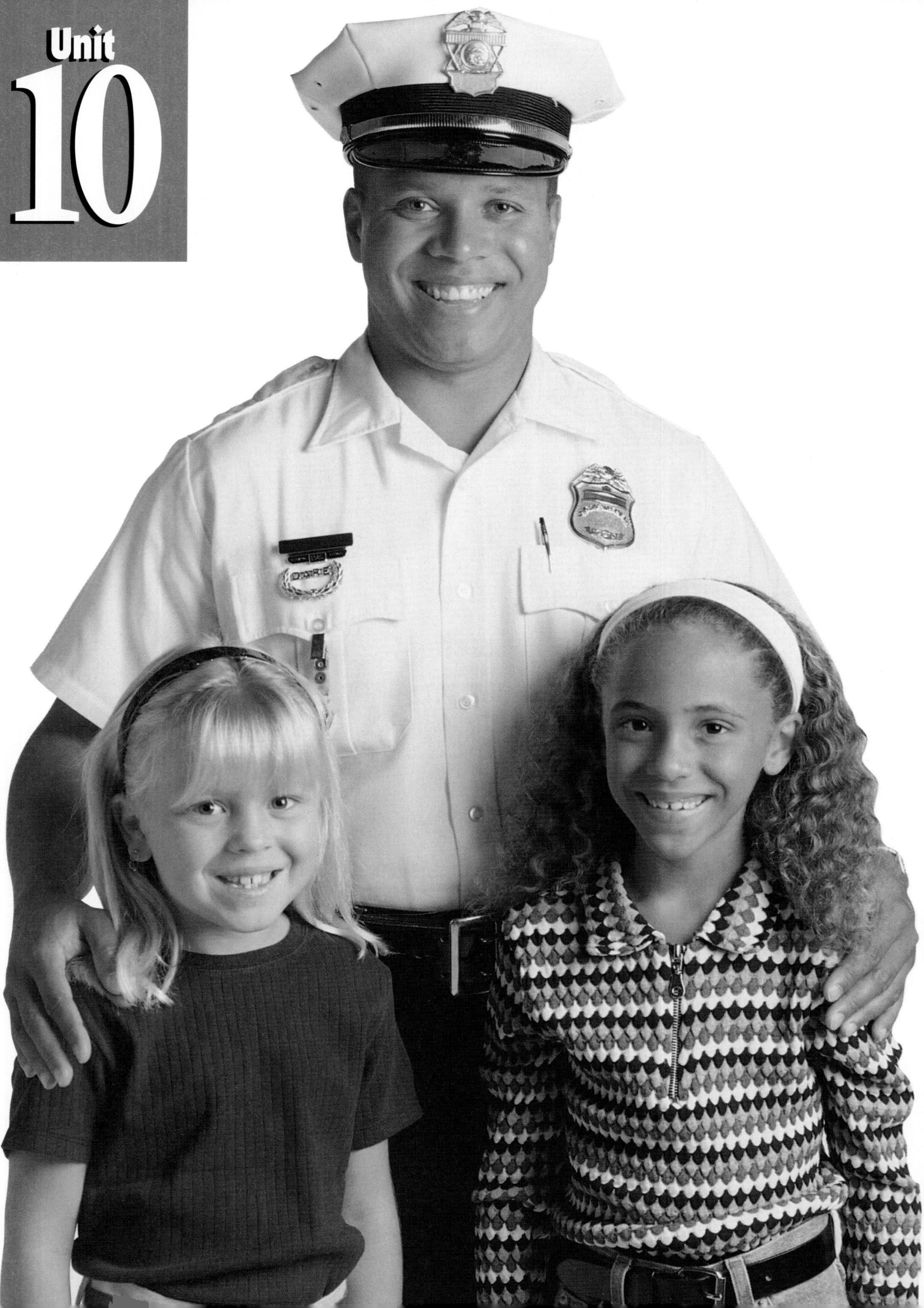

Injury Prevention and Safety

PRACTICE HEALTH STANDARD 4

Think About Why You Do What You Do

Practice this standard at the end of this unit.

1. **Name ways you learn about health.** You learn about health by reading books.

2. **Tell what things help health.** Your teacher tells you about books that help your health.

3. **Choose what helps health.** This book helps your health.

4. **Do not choose what harms health.** Do not listen to a friend who may be wrong.

Lesson 30 Stop, Drop, and Roll

Life Skills

I will follow safety rules for home and school.

I will follow safety rules for bad weather.

What You Will Be Able to Do

Tell safety rules at school.

Tell safety rules in case of fire.

Tell safety rules for a thunderstorm.

Words You Will Learn

A **safety rule** is a rule that keeps you safe.

Stop, Drop, and Roll is what to do if clothes catch fire.

What Are Safety Rules at School?

A **safety rule** is a rule that keeps you safe.

Tell your teacher if you spill something.

Keep things off the floor where people walk.

Do not run in school.

Do not splash water in the restroom.

Do not push and shove on the playground.

What Are Safety Rules in Case of Fire?

Know two ways to leave each room.

Crawl on the floor if there is smoke.

Get out as fast as you can.

Stop, drop, and roll if your clothes catch fire.

Pick a place to meet your family outside.

Do not go back inside.

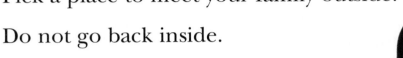

Health Words

Stop, Drop, and Roll is what to do if clothes catch fire.

Activity

Weather Watch

Draw a thunderstorm.

Write one safety rule on your picture.

Safety Rules for a Thunderstorm

- Get inside quickly.
- Stay off the telephone.
- Stay away from water.

Lesson 30 Review

Health Questions

1. What are five safety rules at school? **page 175**

2. What are five safety rules in case of fire?
   page 176

Lesson 31 Safety Town

Life Skills

I will follow safety rules when I play.

I will follow safety rules when I ride in a car.

What You Will Be Able to Do

Tell safety rules for when you bike.

Tell safety rules for when you cross a street.

Tell safety rules for when you swim.

Tell safety rules for when you ride in a car or on a bus.

Words You Will Learn

A **crosswalk** is a place to cross the street.

A **safety belt** is a belt that keeps you in place in a car.

What Are Safety Rules for When I Bike?

Do not ride your bike too fast.

Do not ride your bike in the dark.

Use hand signals.

Do not ride your bike in the street.

Walk your bike when you cross a street.

Watch for traffic when you cross a street.

Traffic is cars, buses, and trucks that are moving.

What Are Safety Rules for When I Cross a Street?

Use a crosswalk if there is a crosswalk.

A **crosswalk** is a place to cross a street.

A crosswalk is marked by lines on the street.

Cross at a corner if there is no crosswalk.

Look left, then right, then left before you cross.

Cross when the sign says walk.

Cross when the light facing you is green.

Cross when the guard signals it is okay.

What Are Safety Rules for When I Swim?

Learn how to swim.

Swim only when a grown-up is watching.

Do not swim by yourself.

Do not eat or chew gum while you swim.

Do not swim far out in a lake or ocean.

My Health Plan

Use the same life skill.
Make your own Health Plan.

Be Safe in a Car

 **Life Skill** **I will follow safety rules when I ride in a car.**

Name _____

Date _____

My Plan: Here are safety rules for when you ride in a car.

- **I will wear a safety belt.**

A **safety belt** is a belt that keeps you in place in a car.

- **I will ride in the back seat.**
- **I will keep my hands and head inside.**

What I Did:

Sunday _I wore a safety belt. I rode in the back seat._

Monday _____

Tuesday _____

Wednesday _____

Thursday _____

Friday _____

Saturday _____

What Are Safety Rules for When I Ride a School Bus?

Mind the bus driver.

Do not yell and scream.

Stay in your seat.

Do not put books in the pathway.

Lesson 31 Review

Health Questions

1. What are six safety rules for when you ride your bike?
   page 179

2. What are six safety rules for when you cross a street?
   page 180

3. What are five safety rules for when you swim? **page 181**

4. What are three safety rules for when you ride in a car?
   page 182

5. What are four safety rules for when you ride the school bus? **page 183**

Lesson 32 Stranger Danger

Life Skills

I will protect myself from people who might harm me.

I will follow safety rules to protect myself from violence.

What You Will Be Able to Do

Tell how to stay safe from a stranger.

Tell what to do if you get an unsafe touch.

Words You Will Learn

A **stranger** is someone you do not know.

Violence is harm done to a person or thing.

An **unsafe touch** is a touch that is wrong.

Who Is a Stranger?

A **stranger** is someone you do not know.

Most strangers are nice.

But some strangers might harm you.

Do not talk to a stranger.

Do not take anything from a stranger.

Do not go anywhere with a stranger.

Yell and run if a stranger bothers you.

Tell your parents or guardian.

Health Words

Violence is harm done to a person or thing.

What Is an Unsafe Touch?

An **unsafe touch** is a touch that is wrong.

Suppose someone touches your body.

The person touches a private body part.

A private body part is covered by a swimsuit.

Yell as loud as you can.

Run away from the person.

Tell a grown-up you trust.

Tell a grown-up about an unsafe touch.

Activity

Badge of Trust

Suppose you get lost.

Ask a grown-up to help you.

Ask a police officer.

Ask a clerk who wears a badge.

1. Draw a badge and cut it out.

2. Write your name on the badge.

3. Write the name of a grown-up you trust.

4. Show your parents or guardians the badge.

Lesson 32 Review

Health Questions

1. What are five ways to stay safe from a stranger?
   page 185

2. What should you do if you get an unsafe touch?
   page 186

Lesson 33
S-A-F-E from Guns and Gangs

Life Skills

I will stay safe from guns.

I will stay away from gangs.

What You Will Be Able to Do

Tell safety rules around guns.

Tell what gangs do.

Words You Will Learn

A **gun** is an object that fires bullets.

A **gang** is a group of people who harm others.

What Are Safety Rules Around Guns?

A **gun** is an object that fires bullets.

A bullet is a small piece of metal.

A gun can harm you.

Suppose you see a gun.

Do not touch the gun.

Do not play with the gun.

Tell a grown-up if you find a gun.

Stay away from anyone who carries a gun.

What Is a Gang?

A **gang** is a group of people that harms others.

Gangs use and sell drugs.

Gangs use guns and knives to harm others.

Gangs steal and write on buildings.

Stay away from gangs.

Say NO if someone asks you to join a gang.

Tell your parents or guardian.

Your parents or guardian will protect you from gangs.

Make Wise Decisions™

Your friend finds a gun.

Your friend dares you to pull the trigger.

Suppose you pull the trigger.

1. Is it safe?

2. Do you show respect for others?

3. Do you follow family rules?

What should you do?

Lesson 33 Review

Health Questions

1. What are four safety rules around guns? **page 189**

2. What are three things that gangs do?
page 190

Lesson 34 A Guide to First Aid

Life Skill

I will learn first aid.

What You Will Be Able to Do

Tell what to do if someone is hurt.

Tell first aid skills for some injuries.

Words You Will Learn

First aid is quick care for a hurt person.

9-1-1 is a phone number to call for help.

An **injury** is a kind of harm to the body.

What Should I Do If Someone Is Hurt?

Suppose someone is hurt and needs first aid.

First aid is quick care for a hurt person.

Send a friend for help or yell for help.

Call 9-1-1 if you cannot find a grown-up.

9-1-1 is a phone number to call for help.

Say your name and where you are.

Tell what happened.

Do what the person on the phone tells you to do.

Activity

First Aid Spelling Bee

Learn the first aid skills in each box.

Each box tells how to care for an injury.

An **injury** is a kind of harm to the body.

Listen to your teacher read each box.

Spell the name of the injury.

Cut

1. Wash the cut with soap and water.
2. Put a clean bandage on the cut.

Nosebleed

1. Sit down and lean forward.
2. Pinch your nose together for ten minutes.

Bee Sting

1. Ask a grown-up to get out the stinger.

2. Put an ice pack on the stung part.

Sunburn

1. Put cool, wet cloths on the burned parts.

2. Cover the burned parts with gauze.

Lesson 34 Review

Health Questions

1. What should you do if someone is hurt?
page 193

2. What are first aid skills for four injuries?
pages 194-195

Unit 10 Review

Health Questions

1. What are five safety rules at school?
   Lesson 30 page 175

2. What are six safety rules for when you cross a street? **Lesson 31 page 180**

3. What are five ways to stay safe from a stranger? **Lesson 32 page 185**

4. What are three things that gangs do?
   Lesson 33 page 190

5. What should you do if someone is hurt?
   Lesson 34 page 193

Health Words

Write the answers on your paper.

crosswalk

gun

injury

safety rule

stranger

1. A _____ is someone you do not know.
   Lesson 32

2. A _____ _____ is a rule that keeps you safe.
   Lesson 30

3. A _____ is a place to cross the street.
   Lesson 31

4. An _____ is a kind of wound. **Lesson 34**

5. A _____ is an object that fires bullets.
   Lesson 33

Make Wise Decisions™

You are riding in a car.

Suppose you stick your head out the window.

- Is it safe?

- Do you follow family rules?

- Do you show good character?

What should you do?

Health Skills

Express Yourself

Make up a rhyme with a bike safety rule.

Learn on Your Own

Practice Stop, Drop, and Roll.

Use Thinking Skills

Why should you stay away from gangs?

Be a Good Citizen

Be able to tell your address and phone number.

Glossary

9-1-1: a phone number to call for help.

A

ad: a message to get you to buy something.

age: to grow older.

alcohol: a drug found in some drinks.

allergy: the body's bad reaction to something.

angry: feeling very mad.

asthma: makes it hard to breathe sometimes.

B

bones: hard body parts.

brain: a body part that tells you what to do.

breakfast: the first meal of the day.

C

cancer: an illness in which harmful cells grow.

cavity: a hole in a tooth.

character: having right actions.

checkup: a check to see how healthy you are.

chores: small jobs.

conflict: a disagreement.

cooperate: to work together.

crosswalk: a place to cross the street.

D

Diet Guidelines: rules for eating.

drug: something that changes how the mind or body works.

drug-free: not to use harmful drugs.

E

entertainment: what you like to see and do.

exercise: to move your muscles.

F

family: people who belong together.

family rules: rules your family makes.

fast food: a food that is served fast.

feelings: the ways you feel inside.

first aid: quick care for a hurt person.

fitness: being in top form from exercise.

flossing: removing food stuck between teeth.

food group: foods that are alike.

Food Guide Pyramid: shows the five food groups.

friend: someone you know and like.

G

gang: a group of people that harms others.

germ: a tiny living thing.

good character: having right actions.

good health: being the best you.

good table manners: nice ways to eat.

grooming: making your body neat and clean.

gun: an object that fires bullets.

H

health: being the best you.

health fact: a true message about health.

healthful entertainment: entertainment that keeps your mind and body healthy.

healthful weight: the best weight for you.

health helper: helps you stay healthy.

health plan: a plan to do a life skill.

heart: a body part that pumps blood.

heart disease: a problem with how the heart works.

heart fitness: having a strong heart.

I

injury: a kind of harm to the body.

L

law: a rule that keeps people safe.

learn: to get to know something.

life skills: healthful actions you do.

litter: trash on the ground or in water.

lungs: body parts that help you get air.

M

medicine: a drug that helps the mind or body.

muscles: body parts that help you move.

N

neighbor: someone who lives near you.

noise: sound that can harm you.

P

pollution: anything that harms the air, water, or land.

posture: the way you sit and stand.

Q

quiet time: time you spend without noise.

R

respect: thinking highly of someone.

rule: a guide to tell you how to act.

S

safety belt: a belt that keeps you in place in a car.

safety rule: a rule that keeps you safe.

say NO skills: ways to say NO.

secondhand smoke: smoke from other people's cigarettes and cigars.

sleep: a time when you are not awake.

smokeless tobacco: tobacco for chewing.

snack: food or drinks between meals.

special: to be very important.

stomach: a body part that changes food.

Stop, Drop, and Roll: what to do if clothes catch fire.

stranger: someone you do not know.

stress: body changes from strong feelings.

sunscreen: a lotion that blocks the sun's rays.

T

tobacco: a plant that has a harmful drug.

U

unsafe touch: a touch that is wrong.

V

vaccine: medicine that keeps germs from harming you.

violence: harm done to a person or thing.

W

warm fuzzy: a nice thing to say or do.

warm up: to get muscles ready to move.

wise decision: the best choice.

wrong decision: a choice with bad results.

Index